Praying with
the Women Mystics

Selected, compiled, and interpreted
by
Mary T. Malone

the columba press

First published in 2006 by
the columba press
55A Spruce Avenue, Stillorgan Industrial Park,
Blackrock, Co Dublin

Cover by Bill Bolger
Cover photo by Shay Doyle
Origination by The Columba Press
Printed in Ireland by ColourBooks Ltd, Dublin

ISBN 1 85607 557 5

Acknowledgements
The author and publisher gratefully acknowledge the kind permission
of the following to use material in their copyright: John Wolters for two
quotations from *Revelations of Divine Love* by Julian of Norwich, trans-
lated by Clifton Wolters; Oxford University Press for quotations from
Gertrude the Great, Hadewijch of Brabant and the Life of Leoba, all
from *Medieval Women's Visionary Literature* edited by Elizabeth Alvilda
Petroff; Continuum International for a quotation from Jean Donovan,
quoted in *Virtuous Magic: Women Saints and Their Meanings*, Sara
Maitland and Wendy Mulford, and published by Mowbray in 1998;
Bear & Co, Vermont, for a quotation from Hildegarde of Bingen's
Scivias translated by Bruce Hozeski; Harper SanFrancisco for a quote
from *The Long Loneliness: An Autobiography* by Dorothy Day, and for the
poem by Frances Croake Frank as quoted in *Freeing Theology: The
Essentials of Theology in Feminist Perspective* edited by Catherine Mowry
LaCugna. If we have inadvertently used other material which is copy-
right we offer our apologies and invite the copyright holder to contact
us so that things can be put right in future editions.

Table of Contents

For Brid and Shirley: your friendship is prayer in my life
And for Francis, teacher of freedom and gardener of my soul

Introduction

These prayer-poems were written in an attempt to communicate the riches of the women mystics of the Christian tradition to a wider audience. These women are, for the most part, unknown in the churches, and with the exception of groups of academics and specialists, the wisdom, brilliance and grace of their spirituality have been forgotten. A few names like those of Hildegarde of Bingen and Julian of Norwich have become more familiar in recent years but, in general, the radical significance of the women's contribution for the future of the church has not been realised. Other women, such as Clare of Assisi and Catherine of Siena are known to some extent within their Franciscan and Dominican communities, but even here the central core of female mystical spirituality has often had little influence on everyday spiritual life.

Between the years of 1150 and 1450, there was an explosion of women's mystical writing expressed in prose, poetry, autobiography, and didactic texts. We know the names of hundreds of women and thousands of pages of their writings have survived. Even this is a miracle because, in many places and at many times, spiritual and theological writing by women was seen as harmful for the Christian community, and often even heretical. Much of this writing was destroyed in inquisitorial fires, ignored as mere fantasy, or the fact of womanly authorship was deliberately suppressed, and the work re-published under male authorship.

These are Christian writings of a most profound significance. They open for us a window into the spiritual lives of Christian women over several centuries. This is nothing like a complete picture of the Christian sensibilities of women – such knowledge has been lost forever – but we are blessed with a sufficient number of fragmentary insights into some lives that we can begin to glimpse what women Christians believed, what they thought and how they prayed in convent, family, beguinage and anchorhold. And we can learn enough to feel gratitude for what has survived and a sorrowful outrage that so much has been lost forever.

For these women's writings open for us a door to the Christian faith of the forgotten female members of the church. The Christian writing that has come down to us has been almost entirely in a male voice. No woman has ever been allowed to influence the theology, official teaching, liturgical ritual, or even the language of these productions in the preceding two millennia of the church's life. All is male reflection on male experience, voiced in male symbolism and male prayer-forms, to a God predominantly imaged and addressed in male terms. This constitutes the church's self-expression to this day. The writings of these women, however, allow us to understand that in all this tradition, profoundly rich though it be, we have just a partial expression of the Christian faith.

There is another tradition, that of the women Christians who have been always a part of the Christian community, but silenced almost completely. Without the writings of these women, we would never know what women have believed, thought, taught or prayed. But now we do know, and what we know is so rich and complex that it would take several lifetimes to decipher. On the other hand, these writings can be understood by every believer, as they were in fact intended by their authors. No woman mystic saw herself as more special or holier than others, but each one saw herself as being required to invite all, especially all women, to pursue the path of mystery.

This is not the place to explore in detail the richness of the women's medieval mystical tradition. Even among specialists, its origin and development are difficult to describe. A few points should be made, however, to clarify the source, context, and significance of these prayer-poems, which stem mostly, but not exclusively from the medieval tradition.

The vast majority of these women writers were single women who were following their Christian vocation in a variety of ways. Most were nuns in the Benedictine tradition, or attached to the newer communities of Cistercians, Dominicans or

Franciscans. For a variety of reasons, such nuns became even more dependent on the clergy for liturgy and spiritual sustenance during the medieval period, and the amply-documented male resistance to such pastoral care may have contributed to the subsequent explosion of women's writing. From these women come works of theological and liturgical significance, often flowing from the liturgical round of the year, and intended specifically for the spiritual formation of the specific community.

There had always been a tradition of men and women living as recluses from the time of desert monasticism in the fourth century, but the practice of women living the life of a hermit flourished throughout Europe, particularly in the thirteenth and fourteenth centuries. Julian of Norwich is but one of the most familiar. From these courageous women come works of profound personal reflection. The women recluses had come to the decision that life was designed for one thing only: the full time seeking of God.

The third group to be mentioned caused wonderment and apprehension throughout the Middle Ages because they constituted a completely new grouping of women in a society where the position of women was strictly defined as *aut maritus aut murus*, that is, either married or enclosed in a convent. These new women were the Beguines. Their origins and history remain shrouded in ambiguity. These were independent women who trespassed beyond the allotted boundaries. They did not marry, did not enter convents, and insisted on supporting themselves by the work of their own hands. They gathered in small groups, organised large and complex living arrangements, or lived as recluses and hermits. These women organised their own spiritual lives and it is from the Beguines that the most innovative and brilliant spiritual writing emerges.

The mystical writing from all three groups has several characteristics in common, but here I will mention but a few of the most relevant. Most of these women wrote in the vernacular languages, thereby making their teaching more accessible and less subject to the control of the clergy, who still saw Latin as the exclusive religious language. Almost without exception, these women mystics wrote of God and addressed God in gendered terms. God was experienced and addressed as Mother as well as

Father, but also as Lady-Love, Woman-Spirit, and Lady Wisdom, as well as in the traditional formula of male symbolic language. All these writings were didactic, that is they were intended to teach others, and women in particular, how to pray, how to enter the realms of mystical union and how to live lives of public compassion. For prayer was never an end in itself, but was intended to lead to a life that would be focused on making God's love influential in people's lives in the exercise of justice and compassion. Finally, this mystical writing demonstrated that these women had come to see themselves in a different light from that portrayed in existing Christian teaching about women. The sense and wonder of having been made in the image of God was predominant in this writing. Women did not feel as if they were following the path of Eve, the origin of sin. They did not feel that their bodies were sinful and the cause of the downfall of the human race. On the contrary, these women felt that they had been ennobled by creation and that the humanity they inhabited had been changed forever by the incarnation. From the humanity of Jesus, they had come to understand and experience their own humanity in a completely new way.

And this brings us to the core of this writing, which is the practice of mysticism by women. The interweaving of humanity and divinity in Jesus and, therefore, since the incarnation, in every Christian, was taken by these women at face value. They felt God-like. They experienced a kind of co-naturality with God. They took it for granted that creation in the image of God had continuous reality in their lives; in fact was the central reality of their lives. As their spiritual journey continued, they came to experience no gap between their humanity and God. The love of God had wiped away all distance. Their hearts were filled with an infinite yearning for closer union with the One in whose image they were made, and in whose love they existed.

Therefore the women sought and experienced a direct access to God. Especially during the celebration of the liturgy, and in the reading of scripture, but also in their everyday experiences of human interaction and in the beauties of nature, they had come to know God. But the women wanted more, more access, more love, more union, and more likeness. Whereas many male mystics felt that the core of mysticism lay in doing the will of

God, the women felt themselves drawn to an experience of identity with God. Many of them, together with Catherine of Genoa, felt enabled to say, 'My real me is God.' From this experience they felt that their lives consisted in simply unfolding the image of God within them. It is in this context that many of the women mystics, and particularly Marguerite Porete, spoke of the experience of nothingness in the presence of God's ultimate reality.

It can be well understood, then, that the women had to search for a new language in which to express this new experience. In one sense, words failed them. In another sense, words flowed from them in brilliant formulations as they tried to discover, with complete integrity, their own appropriate form of inner discourse. Sometimes the traditional liturgical and theological formulae expressed their religious experience. At other times, they found themselves creating wholly new formulations for their new experience of God.

It is precisely here that women today are challenged to follow their example – to find our own appropriate form of inner discourse, so that we can pray with full integrity in words that express the nature and quality of our relationship as women with God. And not only in words – also in silence. The women mystics knew the value of silence, of being wordless, of unspeaking and unsaying everything that had been spoken and said about God. Because in the end, all words are inadequate.

These prayer-poems have been placed in a contemporary setting to try to communicate some of this experience. Some of the prayers (marked with an asterisk) are direct quotations from the writings of a particular mystic. A few of the prayers derive from my own reflections on the mystics in the circumstances of my own life. So often, I discovered that one of these women who lived perhaps a thousand years ago, said exactly what I needed to say. Most of the prayer-poems, however, are interpretations of some of the central themes from the actual writings of the mystics, but rephrased and interpreted in today's language and today's settings. These prayers are liberally sprinkled with words, phrases and images from the original writings, many of which will be readily recognisable. A few prayers from contemporary women mystics have been included, and to these women I want to express my deepest gratitude.

It is my profound wish that these poems will open a door to a largely forgotten part of our Christian heritage, namely the heritage of women. While newspapers report 'falling numbers' and 'emptying churches', perhaps the discovery of the enormous richness of that part of our tradition that has been at best ignored, and at worst actively silenced, will open new veins of womanly Christian wisdom to be mined for the benefit of the whole community.

Biographies

Beatrice of Nazareth, (c. 1200-1268): Beatrice grew up in a middle-class family in the town of Tienen near Louvain, Belgium. Having been taught to read by her mother, she is said to have memorised the psalms by the age of five. She initially joined a community of Beguines (a more informal and less restrictive kind of religious living than the traditional monastic orders for women), but eventually became part of the new Cistercian community called Nazareth. She was prioress of this house for the last thirty years of her life. Beatrice was talented as a calligrapher, manuscript illustrator and author. She is recognised as a mystic and she tried to communicate her spiritual experiences in her main writing, *Seven Manners of Loving*, which was written in the vernacular in order to reach a wider audience. Her focus was on active longing and active loving, and how this resulted in energetic service. Beatrice died in August, 1268.

Catherine of Genoa, (1447-1510): Catherine was born into an influential family and was married off by her brother as a peace offering to a rival family. Her husband's infidelity left her depressed and without focus for about twelve years. Then she experienced a sudden conversion during Lent, 1473, and began to work with the sick in the local hospital. Finally she persuaded her husband to change his life and he became a Franciscan Tertiary. Catherine remained a lay-woman, and had many mystical experiences. She was fascinated with the idea of purgatory, which she saw as part of the 'Dance of love' between God and the individual soul. Her writings include *Dialogue* and *A Treatise on Purgatory*.

Catherine of Siena, (1347-1380): Catherine was one of twins, the twenty-third and twenty-fourth children of Monna Lapa and

Jacopo Benincasa. Her twin and many of her relatives died in the Great Plague which was raging at that time. It is possible that Catherine's miraculous survival was partly responsible for the enormous spiritual hunger that consumed her life and led to her death at the age of thirty-three. Catherine's life was marked equally by intense personal mystical experiences from a very early age, an extraordinary gift for human friendship, which attracted people to her from all walks of life, and a very public role as a church ambassador. She travelled from the papal court, then at Avignon, all over Italy on papal business. Catherine's own goal was to persuade the pope to return to Rome, and in this she succeeded. Many of her letters survive as well as her *Dialogue*, and also her *Life* written by her friend and spiritual guide, Raymond of Capua. The lay-woman Catherine was named a Doctor of the Church on October 14, 1970 at the same time as Teresa of Avila.

Christina of Markyate, (c. 1096-c. 1155): Christina was born into an Anglo-Saxon family in Norman England, and all we really know of her is the extraordinary story of her escape from an imposed marriage and her final achievement of peace as a nun in the community of St Alban's. It is the story of a cruel and abusive mother, a brutal husband, her escape dressed as a man, and her concealment in an underground cellar by a kindly hermit, Roger. Throughout her ordeal, she is comforted by visions of a more kindly mother, Mary, who promised to find her a 'safe place to dwell'. The account of her escape and visions is told in her *Life*, which ends with her safe arrival at St Alban's.

Dorothy Day, (1897-1980): Dorothy was born in Brooklyn, the third of five children to a journalist father and a mother who was described as the 'mainstay of the family'. By the age of sixteen, Dorothy was at university and had 'ceased to believe'. For twenty years she drifted from job to job (mostly journalism and nursing), and from cause to cause in the anti-war movement, and was initially powerfully attracted to communism. At the age of twenty-nine, she gave birth to her daughter, Tamar, and her life turned around. She was baptised into the Catholic Church in 1927. Thereafter, her life's work centred on relieving the oppression of the poor caused, as she saw it, by capitalism, the abuse of power and greed. She was a life-long non-violent pacifist. After she had joined with Peter Maurin, she founded a newspaper, *The Catholic Worker*, which became the pivot around which all their work centred. As a result, dozens of Friendship Houses sprang up all over North America, and to this day, these continue her work, which she summed up as 'bringing Christ back to earth'.

Frances Croak Frank, (Contemporary): Frances was involved in England in the Anglican struggle for the ordination of women. The poem included here became one of the most powerful statements of the significance of the ordination movement.

Elsie Gerber, (Contemporary): Elsie is a Canadian writer, deeply involved in various aspects of the women's spirituality movement.

Gertrude of Helfta, (1256-c.1302): Gertrude (also called 'The Great') was a brilliant woman who spent practically her whole life at the convent of Helfta, having joined at the age of five. She was initially more attracted to the intellectual life and wrote fluent Latin lyrics, but experienced a conversion at the age of twenty-six, which directed her to the mystical spirituality that was so much a part of the life at Helfta. She was a teacher, counsellor, and mediator, as well as a gifted musician, poet and singer. She is one of the few women for whom we have both a biography and an autobiography. On God's authority, Gertrude did not hesitate to assume clerical authority and clerical roles. Her mystical spirituality centered on the Eucharist, on the humanity of Christ, because 'he is what we are', and she is credited with initiating the image of and devotion to the Sacred Heart. Her principal writings can be found in the *Herald of Divine Love*, a compilation of the Helfta community.

Hadewijch of Antwerp, (Thirteenth Century): We know hardly any details about Hadewijch's life, but can assume from her writings that she was widely educated, and became the supervisor and counsellor of a group of Beguines in what is present-day

Belgium. Dozens of her poems and a series of letters have survived, written in her Flemish vernacular, always dealing with
the theme of love. She is acknowledged as one of the most lyrical
poets of her age.

Hildegarde of Bingen, (1098-1179): Hildegarde towered over her
own age and exchanged theological views with (and often challenged) popes, emperors, queens, kings, bishops and abbots, as
well as being Abbess of her own community. As a tenth child,
she had been given as a tithe to the recluse, Jutta of Sponheim,
but as her spiritual fame grew, a community gathered around
her. Hildegarde was a visionary from the age of five and has left
us a series of brilliant paintings of her visions, as well as musical
and dramatic compositions. Her main theological work, *Scivias*,
created her reputation as a prophet, and led to her many preaching tours in the towns and cities along the Rhine. She also wrote
medical and scientific works, and is recognised as one of the
founders of the science of pharmacy. In her eighties, Hildegarde
was excommunicated for refusing to hand over the corpse of a
young man whom she believed to have been falsely accused.
The decision was reversed shortly before her death. Hildegarde
of Bingen is regarded as one of the most brilliant and accom-
plished women of the European Christian tradition.

Hrotsvit of Gandersheim, (932-c.1000): Hrotsvit was a canoness in
a prosperous convent of aristocratic women, and had access to
all the available literature and scholarship of her age. She is con-
sidered to be the first German poet and the first dramatist since
classical times. She set herself the task of correcting what she
saw as pagan ill-informed views of women and, to this end, she
re-wrote pagan classical dramas and popular legends with alter-
nate Christian themes. She was extremely popular in her own
day and it is likely that her plays were performed in the convent
and elsewhere. Some of her dramas have been performed in our
own time.

Hugeberc of Heidenheim, (Eighth century): We know little of
Hugeberc except that she was Abbess of a Benedictine double
monastery and one of the influential Anglo-Saxon nuns who

had responded to the invitation of Boniface to be part of the mission to Germany. The only writing we have is the description of a pilgrimage to Jerusalem made by Willibald, an episcopal relative.

Julian of Norwich, (1343-1413): Despite the fame of Julian today, we are not even sure of her own name. She was a mystical recluse attached to the Church of St Julian in Norwich. Julian's book, *The Showings,* is presented as an answer to prayer and, in the longer version, the product of a life-time of meditation, finally written down in 1393. Julian is esteemed as a brilliant theologian and was named by Thomas Merton as the 'essential theologian for the twenty-first century'. The theme of the 'motherhood of God' is of particular significance in her writing.

Leoba of Bischofsheim, (700-779): Leoba is remembered as one of the principal architects of the church of Germany together with Boniface. She was an Anglo-Saxon Benedictine nun from the convent of Wimbourne in Essex, and became Abbess of a series of German monasteries. Her *Life* was written by Rudolf, a monk of Fulda, and records the words and deeds of a remarkable leader and missionary. She and Boniface were close friends, and Leoba was also welcomed as the dearest friend of the Empress at the court of Emperor Charlemagne.

Macrina, (327-379): Macrina was the eldest of nine in one of the most famous families of the early Christian Church. Her brothers were Basil the Great and Gregory of Nyssa (who wrote her *Life*) and she was a cousin of Gregory of Nazianzus, all three known as Fathers of the church and distinguished theologians at the early church councils. It is clear from her *Life* that Macrina preceded her brothers into Christianity and was influential in their choice of vocation. Macrina and her mother sold their extensive land holdings, freed their slaves, and spent the rest of their lives founding and directing monasteries.

Shirley Majeau FCJ, (Contemporary): Shirley is a Canadian and has worked in education and spiritual formation, as well as spending thirteen years as a missionary in Argentina. Her current interests are Creation and Dream Spirituality.

Marguerite Porete, (Executed June 1, 1310): Marguerite is one of the most compelling figures in the galaxy of medieval mystics. We only know that she was a Beguine in the region of Hainaut and that she insisted on teaching publicly. Her book, *The Mirror of Simple Souls*, was condemned in 1300 but Marguerite refused to be silenced. This book, lost for centuries, is now studied widely and with growing astonishment. Marguerite was burned at the stake in Paris on June 1, 1310, the first Beguine victim of the Paris inquisition.

Mechtilde of Magdeburg, (1208-1282): Mechtilde spent most of her life as an independent Beguine in her home city of Magdeburg, but retired to the convent of Helfta in 1270, when the Beguines began to be repressed by the papacy. Her main work, *The Flowing Light of the Godhead*, is recognised as one of the most influential works in Christian mysticism. Her poetry is lyrical and prophetic and often critical of the clergy.

Brid Murphy, (Contemporary): Brid is an Irishwoman who recently returned to her native Wexford after spending over fifty years as an educator in Canada, where she was highly regarded as a gifted spiritual guide of great influence. In latter years, she has turned her attention to developing the spirituality of wisdom among those who have reached the third age.

Perpetua of Carthage, (Martyred c. 203): Perpetua, in her early twenties, the mother of a young son, together with her slave-girl, Felicity, and several others, were catechumens in the North African city of Carthage. They were preparing for baptism when they were arrested as part of the campaign of persecution by the Roman emperor Sulpicius Severus against new converts. While in prison awaiting execution in the arena by being thrown to wild animals, Perpetua kept a diary describing her fears, her struggle with her pagan father who was trying to save her life, and her healing dreams, which prepared her for such a violent death. This diary, *The Passion of Saints Perpetua and Felicitas*, is the earliest Christian writing by a woman known to us. After Perpetua's martyrdom, it was edited and published, apparently by Tertullian.

Radegund of Poitiers, (518-587): Radegund, a young Thuringian princess, was captured by the Franks and forced to marry their king, Clothar, after he had murdered several members of her family. She eventually escaped, and under the bishop's protection, was ordained a deacon, and founded the great monastery of Poitiers. We have no writings from her own hand, but can glean something of her religious thought from the poetry of her friend the great hymn-writer, Venantius Fortunatus, and her biographer and religious sister, Baudonivia.

Sojourner Truth, (1779-1883): Sojourner Truth spent the first thirty years of her life as a slave, but lived on to enjoy over seventy years as a free woman. She never learned to read or write, but knew practically the whole Bible by heart. She was a life-long social reformer and was one of those who organised the 'Underground Railway' as an escape route to Canada for slaves fleeing from the United States of America. She was a supremely gifted, charismatic and visionary woman and will always be remembered for her brilliant speech at the Convention on Women's Rights in 1851.

Women Missionaries of El Salvador, (Murdered by the military in El Salvador, December 2, 1980): Jean Donovan, Ita Ford, Dorothy Kazel, Maura Clark and Carla Piette were missionaries working with the poor, having between them the care of thousands of people. They delivered food and medical supplies by truck and motor-bike to the peasant workers and held Bible Celebrations where they could. On return trips, they ferried refugees, clergy, the sick and wounded to safety. It was on one such trip that they were stopped, abused, raped and murdered by six guardsmen.

Litany of Holy Women

We call on all the holy women who have gone before us, channels of God's word and givers of God's life. We want to know their stories, celebrate their lives and share their wisdom and, in remembering, to release their power in our lives:

Mary of Nazareth, Mother of Jesus, whose song of praise burst from her lips in the first annunciation of the good news to the poor, the weak, the forgotten and the despised. God will do and has done great things for them, she proclaimed. *We Remember.*

Elizabeth of Judea, who joined her cousin Mary in shouting the praise of God among the Judean hills, and who knew in her very womb that her God was with her. *We Remember.*

Mary of Magdala, first woman believer, and first preacher of the resurrection, who heard and saw and knew that a great new thing had come to pass. *We Remember.*

Thecla of Jerusalem, who persuaded the apostle Paul to accept her as co-apostle in the preaching of the gospel. *We Remember.*

Perpetua of Carthage, who discovered that resistance to the might of Empire is the new name for grace. Newly baptised, she proclaimed to all her fidelity to the gospel. *We Remember.*

Felicity of Carthage, one-time slave girl of Perpetua, who discovered her freedom in becoming a new Christian. *We Remember.*

Scholastica of Monte Casino, who reminded her brother, Benedict, that the Spirit is above the law. *We Remember.*

Hildegarde of Bingen, who knew herself as a feather on the breath of God, and who taught her sisters to dance in their white robes, shout praise with their eyes, and discern the presence of God in the rising sap of every living plant. *We Remember.*

Clare of Assisi, who persuaded a mighty pope that women were his equal, and taught her sisters to move so lightly on God's earth that even the dust would be at peace. *We Remember*.

Hadewijch of Brabant, who saw her God in the ever-receding shore-line, and never ceased reaching for love. *We Remember*.

Mechtilde of Magdeburg, who lived to be a reflector of God's love and God's being. *We Remember*.

Marguerite Porete, who felt that she was swimming like a fish in the vast ocean of God's mysterious being, so that she was one with God and God was one with her. *We Remember*.

Catherine of Siena, who valued human friendship as one of the main experiences of God's presence. *We Remember*.

Catherine of Genoa, who knew that the reality of her Self was the reality of God. *We Rremember*.

Julian of Norwich, who announced to the church the motherhood of God, and preached that love was God's nature, and therefore ours. *We Remember*.

Joan of Arc, who was falsely accused and falsely executed by being burnt at the stake, all because, as a woman, she had listened to the voice of God. *We Remember*.

Isobel Romee, mother of Joan of Arc, who forced a King, a Pope and an Inquisitor to admit that they had made a mistake in the burning of her daughter and then began the process of her canonisation, even though it took another five centuries. *We Remember*.

Teresa of Avila, who re-awakened the spiritual heart of Europe and taught it the journey back to God. *We Remember*.

And all our mothers, grandmothers and foremothers, who handed on to us the wisdom of womanhood and the womanly vision of God. *We Remember*.

May the God who dances in creation, who embraces us in the human love of our friends, who shakes our life with thunder, bless us and send us out to continue our journey toward wise faith, blazing hope and generous love.

Who Am I?

Who Am I?
God of light, I have never known such darkness:
darkness all around me in this cell of death,
and deeper darkness in this cell of my own making.
Aching darkness now, when all that is loved and familiar is lost.
All that I knew of myself is gone;
I do not know what name to call myself.
The name of Mother – my child is gone;
The name of Daughter – my father and mother disowned me,
and even worse, I them;
The name of Citizen - the old familiar rules of life have lost their
power.

But here alone in my unbeing,
alone but for my water-jar,
I cry out to You to rename me.
And then I know.
I feel Your power welling up within.
Your hand strokes my face, again I feel it,
and there is my water-jar telling me the mystery:
a jar is a jar is a jar.

And I?
I can only call myself that which now truly I am.
I have discovered my true name, my only name, my Self.
I am Christian:
and the prison becomes a palace.

(Perpetua of Carthage)

Dream Glimpses

I reach out and cannot touch.
I reach up, and over my head the lip of the fountain glowers.
I hear the running water and my thirst grows deeper.
I am standing here beneath this living water
    and I am dying of thirst.
My face and throat constrict with longing.
And then, it overflows:
a trickle reaches me,
then a stream,
and then a surge.
I bathe my face, my lips, my body in this sweet, sweet flood.

But my soul is dead;
my spirit is shriveled.
My heart is stone deaf.
And then, music:
I see this great silver tree and
    somewhere the music-maker stirs the leaves
and each shiny leaf sings its own song,
a tree-full of harmony.
My soul awakens to this symphony
and the music of eternity floods my soul.
And now again I know myself to have speech of my God.

The fragrance of God's presence feeds again my flagging desire,
and I am surrounded by joy
deep within and in the faces of my friends.
And the green boughs with golden apples
    promise everlasting nourishment.
O Dream-maker, again You whisper my name
    – I am the darling of God.

(Perpetua of Carthage)

My Name is Joy

God, you call out to me,
and I feel your presence like the great swells of the sea.
My soul swims in this sea of joy and delight,
which flows and runs from you.
And then I no longer simply feel joy,
I am Joy.
For you, O God,
Lady Joy and Lady Love,
have transformed me into Yourself.
And now my new name is Joy,
And my new name is Love,
even though I love so little.
For now
I live by Joy and
love by Love.

(Marguerite Porete)

Look at the Birds of the Air (Mt 6: 25-34)

God of Light and Flight,
I look at the soaring birds and my spirit soars toward You.
The birds glide through the air without effort,
not even a wing-beat.
My soaring is more laboured;
mad flutters accompany my feebly flying spirit.

But I know what the birds tell me:
that your love glides and flows toward me without effort.
My gliding lacks grace
but Your gliding love graces my life.

You are the sun of my life, O God,
I am your reflection.
When you shine, I do what I was made to do.
I reflect God.

(Mechtilde of Magdeburg)

*The Hazelnut**

And God showed me something small,
no bigger than a hazelnut,
lying in the palm of my hand,
and I perceived that it was round as any ball.
I looked at it and thought: What can this be?
And I was given the general answer:
It is everything which is made.
I was amazed that it could last,
for I thought that it was so little,
that it could suddenly fall
into nothing.
And I was answered in my understanding:
It lasts and always will
because God loves it;
and thus everything has being
through the love of God.

(Julian of Norwich)

WomanSpirit of God

O Holy WomanSpirit,
from you the clouds have their flowing
the air its movement,
the stones their moisture,
the waters spurting forth in streams
and the earth its glorious green verdure.

My God reveals herself in all her beauty
    in the mirror of creation,
She flames above the fields to signify the beauty of the earth,
the beautiful earthen matter from which we are all made.
She flames on the waters of the world,
suffusing the whole water-fed world,
as life suffuses my body.
She burns in the sun and the moon
to show forth our brightness of intellect
and strength of spirit.
She gleams in the stars to show us
    the words we may use for praise.

And I,
a feather floating on the breath of God,
pray that the Spirit of God
may cleanse me from the malice
that drags me down to earth,
and win me the friendship of God.

(Hildegarde of Bingen)

*Trees of Grace**

I had gone into the courtyard before Prime
and was sitting beside the fishpond
absorbed by the charms of the place.
The crystalline water
flowing through the fresh green trees standing around,
the birds circling in flight,
and above all,
the freedom of the dove gave me pleasure.
There was nothing but sweet calmness.
I was lonely and longing for an intimate companion.
You, O God, guided my prayer,
breathing into me the knowledge
that if I poured back like water
     the flowing streams of your grace,
I would grow in grace like the trees
     when they are in fresh flower,
I would soar easily toward you like the birds
and I would learn to live more in your friendship
and my heart would be free.
I would let go, O God.
Let it be.

(Gertrude the Great of Helfta)

*Woman's Body (1)**

Did the woman say,
When she held him for the first time in the dark of a stable,
After the pain and the bleeding and the crying,
'This is my body, this is my blood'?

Did the woman say,
When she held him for the last time in the dark rain on a hilltop,
After the pain and the bleeding and the dying,
'This is my body, this is my blood'?

Well that she said it to him then,
For dry old men,
Brocaded robes belying barrenness,
Ordain that she not say it to him now.

(Frances Croake Frank)

*Woman's Body (2)**

Do not disdain your body,
For the soul is just as safe in its body
as in the kingdom of heaven – though not so certain.
It is just as daring – but not so strong,
Just as powerful – but not so constant,
Just as loving – but not so joyful,
Just as gentle – but not so rich,
Just as holy – but not so sinless,
Just as constant – but not so complete.

(Mechtilde of Magdeburg)

Ain't I a Woman?*

That man over there says that women need to be helped into carriages and lifted over ditches, and to have the best place everywhere. Nobody ever helps me into carriages or over puddles, or gives me the best place – AND AIN'T I A WOMAN?

Look at this arm! I have ploughed and planted and gathered into barns, and no man could head me – AND AIN'T I A WOMAN?

I could work as much and eat as much as any man – when I could get it – and bear the lash as well – AND AIN'T I A WOMAN?

I have borne thirteen children and seen most of 'em sold off to slavery, and when I cried out with my mother's grief, not but Jesus heard me – AND AIN'T I A WOMAN?

(Sojourner Truth)

My Real Me is God

Mystical audacity amazes me:
no measly-mouthed pieties,
no weasel words
to lure the heart into sham satisfactions;
no pseudo humility
to soothe a cowardly conscience;
no hedging of bets
to get on the safe side of childish fears of God;
no hesitation
to name things, as Perpetua did of old,
just the way they are.

My real me is God,
not hesitating to take Incarnation seriously,
not hesitating to claim their baptismal being,
not hesitating to accept Eucharist at its simplest word,
not hesitating to know the Creator in the midst of creation.

Incarnation:
When God revealed God,
God chose humanity:
My real me is God.

Baptism:
I am named
in the mysterious human-divine flow
of the holy One of God:
My real me is God.

Eucharist:
When Jesus longed for union,
Jesus chose the life-giving bread of humans.
I do Eucharist
and my real me is God.

Creation:
It shouts aloud that God is here
and God is one;
and I swim in the ebb and flow of God's life
and my real me is God.

Oh well they knew that this is
a glimpse
a flash
a word
a hope
a leap of faith.

But they did not look away,
they looked deep within
and what they saw
was their deepest human, created,
     washed, fed and sustained selves;
and they said in wonder,
and yet in homely love:
My real me is God.

(Catherine of Genoa)

Naming God

The Singing Trinity

Have you heard the singing of the Trinity?
the full-throated, robust music
that fills the universal air
with rhythmic trembling,
and ripples along spring-flowering branches
with the delicacy of cherry-blossom.

One voice sings:
I am white water,
a restless surging stream
sparkling, casting light everywhere at once
gurgling with the pleasure
of life and movement
and plunging forward into mystery.

The second voice sings:
I am the running tide
flowing and ebbing,
always in motion, never at rest,
coming and going
divine and human, human and divine,
a tide that runs eternally
with the song of unending love.

The third voice sings:
I am the pulsing of energy
rising as sap
bursting as leaf and flower
redenning as autumn glow,

fading as seasons change,
but always living, feeding, sheltering
and always showering with the truth of beauty,
the beauty of truth
the hidden depths of earth.

And so in chorus
the triune voices mingle their songs
in one great chorus
unbroken, unbreakable, unending chorus.
Listen,
and you will hear
the singing Trinity.

(Mechtilde of Magdeburg)

Alleluia

You are Fire	Alleluia
You are Breath	Alleluia
You are Shelter in the storm	Alleluia
You are Wisdom	Alleluia
You are Darkness	Alleluia
You are Light	Alleluia
You are Friend	Alleluia
You are Lover	Alleluia
You are Mother	Alleluia
You are Earth-Body	Alleluia
You are Energy	Alleluia
You are Father	Alleluia
You are the Rising Sap of Spring	Alleluia
You are Life	Alleluia
You are Death Overcome	Alleluia

(Hildegarde of Bingen)

*Love is What God is**

Would you know God's meaning in this thing?
Learn it well:
Love is God's meaning.
Who showed this to you?
Love.
What did God show you?
Love.
Why did God show it to you?
For love …
And I saw surely that before God made us
God loved us,
and this love has never slackened and never will.
And in this love,
God has done everything.
And in this love God has made all things profitable for us.
And in this love
our life is everlasting.

(Julian of Norwich)

A God Who Gives

God of Love and Life,
the pattern of your presence among us is clear enough:
You give and we receive.
You give with overwhelming generosity,
and we receive with our customary casualness.
You give more than we can ask or imagine,
and we receive, sometimes in wonder.

You give us life and breath, and we receive.
You give miracles of newness, and we receive.
You give rain and sunshine and food, and we receive.
You give yourself in prophetic voice,
and in the most unexpected holy people, and we receive.
You take and bless and break and give, and we receive.

But sometimes you challenge us in overwhelming mystery
        and awesome destruction.
The world shakes on its foundations and we are terrified.
The waters move beyond their bounds and we feel engulfed.
The mountains crush the valleys
        and we cry from the buried depths.

Do not, we pray, allow our hearts to go numb
        when this happens.
Do not, we beg, allow us to give in to a tempting paralysis.
Move us, in those times of dread,
to take our turn as the givers,
so that all may find food and shelter and care and nourishment.
Open our hearts to hear the cries of those who weep,
so that what we have received from you in abundance,
        may be passed on to all.
Help us, O God who is Love,
and O Love who is God,
to love even in our own faltering way.

God of Life and Love,
>the pattern of your presence among us is clear:
You give and we receive;
You challenge and we are afraid.
Be with us as we learn again to see you
>in the giving and receiving,
the generosity and the fear,
the alarm and the hope.
And let us learn to repeat with the psalmist:
God is our refuge and strength, a very present help in trouble.
(Psalm 46:1)

(Julian of Norwich)[1]

---

1. I got the idea for this prayer in a reflection by Walter Brueggeman, p. 33 in *Inscribing the Text: Sermons and Prayers of Walter Brueggeman*, edited by Anna Carter Florence, Fortress Press, 2004. It immediately reminded me of the Parable of the Lord and the Servant in Julian of Norwich.

War God

This God I do not know:
the God of the emperors and presidents and prime ministers,
the God who urges shock and horror,
the God who produces awe-struck fear,
the God who commands the bloody death of innocents,
who remain unnamed, discounted, unnumbered, ignored,
deemed irrelevant, beside the main point of
blood-soaked victory
if it comes.
And does it ever come?

But I begin to recognise the God of forgotten women:
of Hadewijch, who reaches towards the ever receding shores;
of Marguerite Porete, who ached back to where she was
      before she was;
of Julian, who knew her God as homely and courteous
      and closer than hands and feet;
of Catherine, who enfolded God in the embrace of friends;
of Hildegarde, who danced and sported with God
      in sap-filled and wind-tossed greenery;
and of so many other women and men of faith
who looked into the face of a courteous God
and knew for that one breathless pause
the moment of adoration.

More Than a Father

The name of Father I have always known,
this God who creates and holds,
this God who calls and welcomes,
this God who rules and loves,
this God whom I once feared and fought.

But Father is not enough to contain the coming God of my being.
As I grow, God grows.
Deep in my being I know a God who is more,
more than Father.
I now know my God as mother.

I have been held in her embrace
I have played at her knee
I have found a home in her heart
I have laid my head on her breast
I have touched the lines on her face
I have looked into her eyes
and I have known
a God who is Mother.

Mother God,
Father God,
keep me in your embrace.

(Mechtilde of Magdeburg)

No Time for Silence

We had been silent for so long,
speaking a language of
half
truths
that told us who we were
and who we could
become.
the icons
became
idols
as we closed our eyes
and clasped our palms in veneration
hallowed
and blessed them
made them food
for our bodies our souls
now
we are reading the Scriptures
for ourselves
sounding out the dark hollow words
that rebirth us
renaming ourselves
and renaming
GOD
in the stained
glass
we see the blood and water
we are speechless
with a new
silence.

(Betty Govinden)

New Beginnings

Spirit of Life, bless us as we enter this new time,
and as we bless one another in peace.
In this time of hope we wish to affirm life for all.
We commit ourselves again
to bring your hope of freedom
to all who suffer despair.
Fill us with a thirst for your justice
and teach us to move beyond
reliance on empty promises and false hopes.

Spirit of Life, renew our vision of a different possibility,
a different world.
Open the eyes of those who are fed
to the cries of the hungry.
Move the hearts of those who are whole
to offer healing to those who suffer.
Turn our eyes inward and outward
to the beauties within and without.
Help us to care for your presence
in the sap-filled plants, in the soaring birds,
    in the murmuring ocean,
in the gurgling streams with their families of fish,
and in our own hearts,
often broken, sometimes healed.

Spirit of Life, renew our dreams.
Help us to attend to your voice
and to know your call amid all the others.
Repair our dreams for the future
when they have become ragged.

Bless all the women of the future,
and grant them loving and listening friends and family.
Open for them a way of peace
so that their children and their children's children
may receive an inheritance
of womanly grace and hope.
Amen, We Pray. Amen.

(Hildegarde of Bingen)

The Happy Hour

Over the centuries the phrase leaps out:
It was the happy hour!
Gertrude is speaking of the happy hour
just after Compline, at the close of day,
the moment when her conversion was begun.

My mind is full of happy hour at the local – any local,
when the day is done and the workers gather at the close of day,
with all the chatter of daily events.
All the now smoke-free aromas of a pub happy hour
in any Irish pub fill my imagination.
And back and forth my spirit roves
between the happy hour at Helfta
and the happy hour in any pub, Ireland.

Happy hour at Helfta was a quiet place and a quiet time
'I saw God there' says Gertrude
'Clearer than any light,
Deeper than any recess,
God came to me
As a beautiful sixteen year old youth.'

God noticed her sadness and said:
'Have you no counsellor that you are sad?'
'O Loving God of the Poor', she replied,
'I am sad because you have made me care
about what passes within my heart.'

In her heart she had seen
the rust of sin staining the pure gold of God's creation.
And she prayed
that the pure gold of Godlikeness
would gleam again within her, rust-free,
and would be etched on her heart
like a seal on soft wax.

'And O God', she said, 'You embraced me
Like a necklace of gold and rose
Seen through crystal.'
Here was the moment of learning God's talent for intimacy,
of being glad and not sad to attend to
what was happening in her heart.

And I cannot help thinking
that somewhere during the happy hour
God, in a necklace of gold and rose,
seen through crystal
is sparkling in an Irish pub
and yet again inviting all and sundry
to enter her talent for intimacy,
and care with gladness
about what happens in her heart.

(Gertrude the Great of Helfta)

The Pilgrim

Walking My Spirit

I set out on the eve of the summer solstice;
my face was set toward the east.
Jerusalem called to me
and all unwillingly,
I pointed my feet along the path they must travel.

My spirit was sluggish, thuggish, dragging me back
but my feet obeyed me more readily.
'Take your spirit for a walk', they said
'feet first and your spirit will follow.'

And it happened:
I saw the bees flitting through the fields
doing what you, O God, had written into their being,
and I knew that you, O travelling God,
would be my journey's companion.

I saw the fields purple with violets,
I saw the buttercups reflecting the light of God's face.
My being seemed to blend together in one mighty purpose,
my spirit and I
feet and soul
were walking in new harmony
towards our God.

(Hugeberc of Hildesheim)

*The Shore**

I swim towards the shore
only to find
that you have enlarged the sea.
You leave me dazed with more desire
and give me more muscle
to swim again towards you.

(Hadewijch of Brabant)

God's Game

You only ever,
They told me, my spiritual guides,
See the behind of God.
You won't catch up with God.
And I,
Who desired a face to face encounter
Felt cheated by them and by God,
and thought I might, perhaps, prove them all wrong.

Then I met Hadewijch in her Godward swimming
and together with her,
saw the receding shore,
felt the deepening desire,
muscled my way forward,
and thought the swim worth the wait.

God of boundless horizons,
I reach toward you
What words are there?
I long, I pine, I ache,
I desire, I thirst,
even I demand.

Now I know that it is all about longing,
longing and just breathing.
God of my every breath,
I gasp and drink deep of the breath of life.
Swimming along,
I draw in huge lungfuls of cool refreshing air.
I want to be sated with spirit.
But I have learned to take it gently,
every dawning day, easy does it,
in and out, in and out.

God of the great receding edges of my dreams,
God of the deep mysterious waters of my self,
One thing I ask:
keep me from skimming the surface.

(Hadewijch of Brabant)

I Miss Eve

I try to name my pilgrim companions,
those who walked, talked, challenged,
those who opened doors,
pulled the rug out from my dawdling feet,
those who pointed out and up and beyond and down deep,
so many.

Until now, lurking behind them all,
has been Eve,
the icon of the seductive, temptable, gossipy woman
the reason for my dimness, my stone-walling,
    my serpent-like explanations.

I could blame her, attack her, shift the weight of shame unto her.
I could lower my hopes,
pull in my horns,
seek safer waters,
aspire to smaller victories.

She had become my prescribed, my comfortable companion.
But now I miss her.
My new companions seek further afield;
there is no stopping Julian or Mechtilde or Beatrice.
They recognise no boundaries, no limits, no excuses,
they give me no comfort zone;
they never heard of reaching beyond your grasp;
they want it all.
They love for good, for all.
They have no backward glances.

So I miss Eve,
my iconic excuse.
I bid her farewell.
I feel my edenic time is over,
and I can begin to face
a boundless place ,
a homeless place,
a desert place,
a peopled place,
an ever-changing place.
And I can begin to call
this new journey
my home.

On Mission

A Great Band of Women

Off to Germany they went, this great band of women,
leaving, without a backward glance, their home convent
   in Wimbourne.
Who were they? Whence came they?
We know some of the names:
their leader, the mighty Leoba,
and with her went, I am told, her disciples,
   Agatha, Thecla, Nana and Eolaba.
I name them with awe,
   these women Christian ancestors of mine,
about whom I know nothing but their names.

But as I read, I learn more.
I seem to know them intimately,
their longings, their excitement, their thirst, their fear.
They were off on a mission.
They were leaving home,
they had been given a voice,
they had been given a purpose.

Their task was to name their God,
to speak abroad their God.
They knew well their call,
as so many women in those darkening times:
build a place of hospitality, of healing, of welcome;
build a home for the homeless,
make a way-station for the wanderer.

And as the light of learning was dying,
make a learning place for those who sought the God of mystery;
make a place of prayer for those who longed for peace,
for those whose troubled souls cried for the touch of hope.

Leoba, they tell me, was a reader, morning, noon and night.
Even as she rested, they read to her,
and if the reader lagged, Leoba was instantly awake.

Leoba stood tall with God's authority.
She strode into the storms of life
    with her cloak flung out behind her.
She gathered up the sins of the community,
    inside and outside the convent,
and living out her name, Leoba, beloved of God,
she met the collective sin of the world
with the collective holiness of her sisters.
Such was the great band of women
    who met their God far from home.
Again I name their names:
    Leoba, Agatha, Thecla, Nana, and Eolaba
and all their nameless sisters.
We meet them in our hearts.
With them we praise our God.

(*Life of Leoba* by Rudolf of Fulda)

El Salvador*

I could almost leave El Salvador
except for the children,
the poor bruised victims of this insanity.
Who would care for them?
Whose heart could be so staunch
    as to favour the reasonable thing
in a sea of their tears and loneliness?
Not mine, dear friend, not mine.

(Jean Donovan).

So they Laid Her Out

So they laid her out
She was the first one
She was so disfigured
her face was so disfigured
the bullet collapsed the bone structure of her face
you couldn't really be sure it was Jean.
Then they pulled the next body out
I think it was Maura
They pulled her over to the side
some of the people came over
and broke branches off the trees
and covered the two bodies.
I remember the stench was terrible.
They pulled up Dorothy.
She was dressed in jeans
but the jeans were on backwards.
The campesinos found them without their jeans on.
They put the jeans back on.
And then they brought up Ita.
It was like bringing up a child.
Her body was crumpled and broken.
Then they laid them all out there
and the people covered the bodies with branches.

(Evidence given by Patricia Lansbury, American consul to El
Salvador about the murder of Jean, Ita, Maura, Dorothy on 2
December 1980)

*Soup Bowls**

I have had to stop myself sometimes.
I have found myself rushing from one person to another
soup bowls and more soup bowls,
plates of bread and more plates of bread,
with the gratitude of the poor
like a loud din in my ears.
Then I realised that this is dangerous work.
To want to help people is a grave temptation.
Maybe we are just helping ourselves by helping others.
This is a long loneliness.

(Dorothy Day)

God Made Me A Priest

Poor Gertrude,
triply silenced in a Christian cocoon of misogyny.

You are Eve, daughter of Satan:
your mouth speaks only evil.

You, a woman, are under obedience:
your voice is irrelevant,
your superiors speak for you, if speech is necessary,
which from women is rarely so.

You are less than nobody in God's church:
was it not you, a woman, who dealt with the devil,
and caused sin to grow and
drag down forever the church of God?
You caused the death and suffering of Jesus
now take your place submissively as an evil irrelevancy.

But God said to Gertrude:
Write, speak, forgive sins in my name:
I will never let your words be in vain,
I now make you a priest of God,
you are my mouth-piece.
My words are your words and yours mine.
The words of the powerful are shallow
like pebbles in an empty can.

I now touch your mouth,
Today I make you my priest
Feed the people,
Bless the bread,
Share the wine.
Speak for me to them.

Remove their doubts and scruples
Lift their burdens
Help the women to stand tall
Tell them 'Come.'

No wonder we call her Gertrude the Great,
Ordained by God herself,
spokesperson of the Holy One.
God of Gertrude,
Gertrude of God,
Touch our mouths with courage,
Loosen our tongues to speak,
Straighten our backs to stand tall,
Priest us! Priest the women,
God the Great, Gertrude the Great.

(Gertrude the Great of Helfta)

Seeking God

Seeking in Seeing

Seeking God is as good as seeing God.
Who, but a saint,
could know so clearly
that the journey is the reality,
the steps are sight,
the effort is reward,
the seeing is the searching,
the dream is the reality?
Seeking God is seeing God.

(Julian of Norwich)

Jumping Sideways

The numbers of lapsed, I read, are leaping ahead;
Year by year, 'those who have fallen away' grow in numbers.
Churchmen – always the men – bewail the faithless ones.
Crisis time has come:
'If only', they say, 'they knew what they are missing.'

Perhaps, I think, they didn't lapse.
Perhaps, like me, they just jumped sideways.
Perhaps the cornered, much-defined God of celibate men
no longer suffices for opening hearts and minds,
for questioning spirits and love-drained souls.

Suppose we asked the women:
'What think you of God?
What God breaks and heals your woman's heart?
What woman-faced God
peers into the depths of woman-being
and awakens echoes of integrity,
echoes of prayer that ring with truth?'

What if, I wondered,
what if women trod the forgotten paths?
What if the old old voices
were raised again,
voices raised to a new face of God
by an old race of women?
What if the Woman-God of Woman-Christians mattered?

What if we proclaimed again:

The Woman-Spirit God of Hildegarde
and her Lady-Wisdom God,
who breathed God-knowledge into the sisters at Bingen?

The Mother God of Julian,
who is courteous and homely and knows no anger?

The God who is Lady-Love,
beloved of Marguerite
who led her on beyond the human-divine divide?

The laughing God of Hadewijch,
whose laughter makes no appearance
in all the tomes of learned men?

The dancing God of Mechtilde,
who laughed and leapt
and invited all to follow?

The sweet-smelling God of Gertrude,
whose perfume penetrated every corner of life?

The friendly God of Catherine,
who made friendship the core of a well-lived life?

The poor God of Clare,
who wished for nothing but to share this poverty?

The heart-broken God of Christina
who healed the scars of cruelty?

The strong-voiced woman God of Hrotsvit,
who urged her to move
    beyond the ancient silencing of women.?

And the fierce God of Perpetua,
who looked into the face of violent death
and recognised a life beyond life?

And the human/divine face of Catherine's God,
who mirrored her self to herself
in the mystery of shared human/divine life?

This is not falling away.
This is leaping for joy.

*Sophia, WomanGod**

When God established the heavens I,
Sophia, WomanGod, was there
When God drew a circle on the face of the deep,
When God assigned to the sea its limit ...
When God marked out the foundations of the earth,
Then I was beside him like a master-worker
And I was daily God's delight, rejoicing before him always,
Rejoicing in the inhabited world
And delighting in the human race.

(Proverbs 8:27-31)

*Sophia in Splendour**

For Sophia is the splendour of eternal light
And immaculate mirror of God's majesty,
And image of God's goodness ...
For she is more beautiful than the sun,
And above all the order of the stars.
Compared with the light, she is found before it ...
Therefore she reaches from end to end mightily
And orders all things sweetly.

(Wisdom, 7:26-8:11)

*God the Wisdom-Woman**

For this is the Wisdom-Woman of God.
She watches over all people and all things.
She is of such radiance and brightness,
That you cannot gaze on her face or on the garments she wears.
For she is awesome in terror and gentle in goodness.
She has the radiance of divinity in her face.
She is with all and in all and of beauty so great
That no one can know how sweetly she bears with people,
And with what unfathomable mercy she treats them.

(Hildegarde of Bingen)

The Abyss of Omnipotence

I do not like the word omnipotence,
power to the max, you might say.
We know the powerful ones:
their faces fill the news, the papers, the gossip sheets;
their names are ever linked with the words of power;
wealth, corporate decisions, corruption, secrecy.
And yet they speak eternally
of transparency, honesty, openness, clarity,
and especially of democracy, the people's good.

But this other omnipotence,
the omnipotence of mystic speech,
is the omnipotence of the abyss,
is emptiness,
is darkness luminous,
is abysmal,
is the entire omnipotence of the Holy One.

Abandon the edges.
Stop skimming the surface.
Seek the abyss.
Face the fear of nothingness,
because here no-thing-ness
is the secret of everything.

This is the secret of your humanity,
of the humanity of the Holy One of God.
This is the gift of woman-humanness.
Infinity is my co-nature,
I am made for this:
Seek infinity – this is your home.

Seek infinity, seek the abyss;
this is also your burden.
Nothing else will satisfy,
but the mysterious Eucharistic depths.

God of the deeps,
this one thing I have learned:
love is not repose.
Just when I am at rest
in the safe boundaries of recognised deeps,
Love comes
and bursts the banks.

God engulfs me again
in a flood of Godness.

(Hadewijch of Brabant)

Why Not Soar?

You have the wings of longing,
You know the pull of hope,
You feel the flowing of desire:

So why not soar?

Fish cannot drown in water,
Birds cannot sink in air,
You cannot fall from my sight:

So why not soar?

Woman, I have adorned you,
Woman, I have delighted in you,
Woman, I have made my home within you:

So why not soar?

Be as the dove, I soar in her.
Lighten your heart, I soar in you.
Uplift your being, be an Easter song:

Why not soar?

(Mechtildde of Magdeburg)

God in the Slaney

Some Sundays
I go looking for God
on the new quays
in old Wexford.

I always have Marguerite in mind.
Look at the Seine, she said;
it rises and takes its travels
through field, town, forest,
and finally reaches Paris
on its way to the sea.
All the time it is called the Seine.
That is its name.

Then the miracle happens:
the Seine reaches the sea
and the Seine loses its own name.
It becomes nameless,
as it mingles
water with water in the vast moving sea.
And no one can tell
where the river ends and the sea begins.

And so it is with me, she mused.
I have my own name,
my journey through life,
my travels,
and then, in my seeking,
like the river,
I enter the vast moving sea of God
and no one can tell
where I end and God begins.

There I am, God and I,
my nameless self lost
in the vast sea of God's presence.
And who can tell, then,
where God ends and I begin?

And so, on some Sundays,
I look at the Slaney,
following its own course
from Lugnaquilla to the sea,
Through Wicklow hills
and Carlow towns
and Wexford farms,
past Enniscorthy Castle and Cathedrals
and so on to Wexford,
where its waters mingle with the sea
and then it is Slaney no more.

And there, standing on the quay,
I try to see myself, as Marguerite did,
lost and unnamed and mingled in God,
freely swimming in a sea of divinity,
not knowing nor needing to know
where humanity ends and God begins
where I end and God begins.

Sometimes, then, I turn town-ward
with my back to the Slaney-sea
and gaze the length of the quays,
from Crescent Pool,
past mussel boats,
to the graceful low-slung bridge.
and there,
right in the middle of the quays,

I try to imagine a woman
being burned to death
on the Wexford quays,
just as Marguerite was
right there in the middle of the Place de Greve
in her beloved Paris,
on the first day of June
in the year thirteen-ten.

How to imagine such a horror.
How to imagine the fear that one lone woman
could evoke in the fierce, fiery, fear-filled church.

Was it because she spoke of swimming in divinity?
Was it because her chosen name for her God
was Lady-Love?
Was it because, as a woman,
she dared to teach about her Woman-God of Love?

How could they have been so terrified
of this one woman, Marguerite,
whose calm acceptance of her horrific death
silenced the on-lookers into awed reverence?

That day, the Seine provided no answers,
and today, turning again toward the sea-bound Slaney,
I seek, not answers,
but some small share of her God-lost self,
some sense of her all-embracing briny divinity,
some feeling that here,
in Wexford, between Slaney and sea
I will learn to keep looking
and not miss the great moment of mingling.

(Marguerite Porete)

Praying Pain

*A Story and a Prayer**

There was a certain poor little crippled girl who sat near the gate of the monastery begging alms. Every day she received her food from the abbess's table, her clothing from the nuns and all other necessities from them; these were given to her from divine charity. It happened that after some time, deceived by the suggestions of the devil, she committed fornication, and when her appearance made it impossible for her to conceal that she had conceived a child, she covered up her guilt by pretending to be ill. When her time came she wrapped the child in swaddling clothes and cast it at night into a pool by the river which flowed through that place. In this way she added crime to crime, for she not only followed fleshly sin by murder, but also combined murder with the poisoning of the water.

When day dawned, another woman came to draw water and, seeing the corpse of the child, was struck with horror. Burning with womanly rage, she filled the whole village with her uncontrollable cries and reproached the holy nuns with these indignant words: 'Oh what a chaste community! How admirable is the life of nuns, who beneath their veils give birth to children and exercise at one and the same time the function of mothers and priests, baptising those to whom they have given birth. For, fellow citizens, you have drawn off this water to make a pool, not merely for the purpose of grinding corn, but unwittingly for a new and unheard of kind of baptism. Now go and ask those women, whom you compliment by calling them virgins, to remove this corpse from the river and make it fit for us to use again. Look for the one who is missing from the monastery and then you will find out who is responsible for this crime.'

At these words all the crowd was set in uproar and everybody, of whatever age or sex, ran in one great mass to see what had happened. As soon as they saw the corpse, they denounced the crime and reviled the nuns.

When the abbess (Leoba) heard the uproar and learned what was afoot she called the nuns together, told them the reason, and discovered that no one was absent except Agatha, who a few days before had been summoned to her parents' house on urgent business: but she had gone with full permission. A messenger was sent to her without delay to recall her to the monastery, as Leoba could not endure the accusation of so great a crime to hang over them. When Agatha returned and heard of the deed that was charged against her, she fell on her knees and gazed up to heaven, crying: 'Almighty God, who knowest all things before they come to pass, from whom nothing is hid and who hast delivered Susanna from false accusations when she trusted in Thee, show Thy mercy to this community gathered together in Thy name and let it not be besmirched by filthy rumours on account of my sins; but do Thou deign to unmask and make known for the praise and glory of Thy name the person who has committed this misdeed.'

On hearing this the venerable superior, being assured of her innocence, ordered them all to go to the chapel and stand with their arms extended in the form of a cross until each one of them had sung through the whole psalter, then three times each day, at Tierce, Sext and None, to go round the monastic buildings in procession with the crucifix at their head, calling upon God to free them in His mercy, from this accusation. When they had done this and they were going into the church at None, having completed two rounds, the blessed Leoba went straight to the altar and, standing before the cross, which was being prepared for the third procession, stretched out her hands towards heaven, and with tears and groans prayed, saying: 'O Lord Jesus Christ, King of Virgins, Lover of chastity, unconquerable God, manifest Thy power and deliver us from this charge, because the reproaches of those who reproached Thee have fallen upon us.'

Immediately after she had said this, that wretched little woman, the dupe and the tool of the devil, seemed to be surrounded by flames, and calling out the name of the abbess, confessed to the crime she had committed. Then a great shout rose to heaven: the vast crowd was astonished at the miracle, the nuns began to weep with joy, and all of them with one voice gave expression to the merits of Leoba and of Christ our Saviour.

So it came about that the reputation of the nuns, which the devil had tried to ruin by his sinister rumour, was greatly enhanced, and praise was showered on them in every place. But the wretched woman did not deserve to escape scot-free and for the rest of her life she remained in the power of the devil.

(Life of Leoba, 700-779 CE)

A Prayer for 'Poor Little Crippled Girls'

Almighty God, God of Leoba,
    the mighty miracle-working Abbess,
Raped God, God of the nameless 'poor little crippled girl',
All-holy God, God of Agatha,
    proved whole and holy in her virginity,
Ravaged God, God of the raped and wretched woman,
    'given over to the power of the devil',
Righteous God,
    God of the indignant voice of public opinion,
Just God, God of the silent, accused, battered, voiceless,
    and mauled ones:

Almighty, All-holy and Righteous,
we recognise this God from Bible and Liturgy
    and hymned invocation;
Raped, Ravaged and Just, we know too this Godly face
in lamentation and sorrow and hope for healing.

But where is the God with a woman's heart
who enters the despair of 'poor little crippled girls'?
Where is the Woman-God
of abused, battered and abandoned women,
who can reach beyond all-holiness
to enter the world of holy pain?

Where is the God of many voices and many names
who speaks for the nameless,
    voiceless, homeless and silenced ones
to share their despair?
Is there such a God?
I know in my woman's bones that if there is not,
then there is no God.

Prayer of a Raped Princess

I can still hear all their voices:
You only get what you deserve.
That will teach you.
Why did you not just give in and obey him?
That is what you get for antagonising him.
How often have you been told that women are to be Selfless …?

God, what is this Self that I am supposed to lose?
Is it the Self made in your image?
Is it the centre of my soul?
Is it the very part of me that I hold dearest –
the Self that seeks your face?
The Self that always hoped to portray your presence?
The Self that Venantius, my dear friend,
    urged on to mysteries beyond speech?

Or is it the Self that now lies battered, violated, wounded?
Now I know what being Selfless is all about;
the core of my being has been laid waste
like fields after the armies have passed through the countryside.

But deep within I know that a new Self is taking shape,
a Self that begins to heal and grow and be nourished.
There is a place I shall never be again.
I know that wherever I go,
whatever I do,
there is a part of me that cannot be touched
    by Clothar's vile lust.

God of raped women, I cry to you,
let this acorn of a new self
grow strong like the greening oaks of my new convent home.

I thank you for the care of my sisters.
I thank you for the healing power
    of the friendship of Bishop Venantius.
I thank you for the healing power
    of the monastic peace here in Poitiers.

Never again will I acknowledge
the false power of brutal princes.
Never again will I doubt
the immense power of my healed and re-awakened Self.
Never again will I forget
that the God of Venantius' hymns
    who marches forth with soaring banners,
is also the God who knows the heart of a raped woman,
who heals the heart of a woman
learning again to trust;
and who touches with gentle love this broken body
and teaches me to cherish the beauty of this Self, this Body,
which images always and forever, divine beauty.

(Radegund of Poitiers)

Prayer of an Abused Daughter

'O God, my true Mother, if only I were allowed to gaze fully at your face.'
(Christina of Markyate, 1096-1160)

'I care not who rapes her as long as someone does.'
(Beatrix, mother of Christina)

God, do you know, can you know what rage is?
Can you see and know the rage of a mother?
Can you feel, in the depths of divine being,
the fury of a mother directed against you?
Because I need you to know this;
I need to know that you know,
or how else am I to survive?

Day in, day out, I cannot stop crying.
I cry because I hurt in my body, from head to toe.
I cry because my spirit is bruised beyond repair.
I cry because I have lost myself.
I seem to have slipped away in a sea of pain.

She loosed her fury against me, her own daughter.
She wanted to destroy my deepest self, so she said.
Were you there? Did you see?
One day at a banquet, she dragged me by the hair,
beat me till she tired of it,
tore my clothes to shreds,
then dragged me back
    as an object of ridicule before all the guests.

I was numb with pain, grief, anguish.
These were my friends, neighbours, and visitors.
All were invited to maul me as they wished.

God, I knew then and I know now
    that these wounds do not heal.
The body's hurts are covered over,
but the spirit takes many lifetimes to restore itself to wholeness.
Even today, so many years later,
    I am deeply, deeply troubled by these memories.

But there have been friends who have shielded me
    from my mother's rage.
When your voice, O God, seemed silent,
and your face, O God, seemed turned away,
one friend always calls me his 'Sunday daughter',
and ignores the danger to himself
    of trying to raise me up to a new joy.

He it is who urged me to turn again, O God, to you:
O that you would turn your face to me.
I prayed to see the face of a good mother,
and you sent your own mother to me.

She was seated near the altar in St Mary's Church.
The priest pointed her out to me – this was my vivid dream.
I gave her a blooming branch of spring flowers.
She handed it back to me and said:
'How is it with you?'
'Ill, my Lady', I said.
My ever-flowing tears prevented me from saying more.
All I wanted was to gaze on a motherly face:
    the face of a kind mother.
She told me I would be delivered.
I wanted more than words – I had heard enough words.

Suddenly something inside me,
like a small bird full of life and joy,
struck my inward parts with its weak fluttering.
And then I felt it flying upwards through my throat

and forming these words:
'Arise Christina, escape is at hand.'
And that day I escaped, dressed and disguised as a man,
wearing man's clothes, and sitting astride the horse as a man.

As I set off across the meadow of hope,
    Psalm 38 flooded my soul:
'God, all my longing is known to you;
My sighing is not hidden from you.'

And then I knew what it was to be a Sunday daughter.

(Christina of Markyate)

We Lost Our Best Friend

God, she taught us to call you the giving one
and now you have shown yourself as the taking one,
in taking her from us.
She who was our light is gone,
it is all darkness with us now.

She brought us gold and silver,
not of coin but of goodness and love.

God, give back love.

She brought us flowering vines and leafing plants
in the gardens of our hearts,
She awakened our desires for you.

God give back desire.

She brought us fields flung with riotous blossoms,
as she showed us the multifaceted dimensions of your light.
Now our eyes are dim with tears.
The light of our life and of our fields is gone.

God give back light.

She gave us the sweet violet, the blushing rose,
    and the gleaming lily.
She showed us the beauty of the land
and of the landscape of the soul.
Now all is arid and weariness.

God give back beauty.

She spoke to us in words of joy and challenge and truth.
She brightened our world with pleasure
    as the moon gleams against the darkness.
She herself walked in truth and now all truth is gone.

God give back truth.

(Mourning for Radegund of Poitiers)

Food for the Hungry

Every noon at twelve
in the blazing heat
God comes to me
in the form of
two hundred grams of gruel.

I know Him in every grain,
I taste Him in every lick,
I commune with Him as I gulp,
for He keeps me alive, with
two hundred grams of gruel.

I wait till next noon
and now know he'd come:
I can hope to live one day more,
for you made God to come to me as
two hundred grams of gruel.

I know now that God loves me –
not until you made it possible.
Now I know what you're speaking about
for God so loves this world
that He gives His beloved Son
every noon through You.

(Anonymous)

Woman God of Love

The Nameless Nights

Woman God of my heart,
it is you I know,
you who beckon me into the nameless nights.
By day I scrabble for love
as the little birds of winter scrabble for grain.
But in the night of unfaith,
the long nameless night,
it is you,
Woman God of love,
it is you,
Woman love of God
that dares me
to open my soul to your womanly caress,
to expand, blossom, breathe
in the darkness.

Woman God of my Life,
you summon me to newness.
Don't let newness escape.
She the Lover comes,
She the Lover goes.
Don't seek stability in this love
but know that only in this love
will you meet the Woman-being of God
and stroke the Woman-face of God

Reason has taught me to seek God
where God is not,
in the given names and images and symbols,
in creeds and dogmas and commands.
But Love, the dark being of new love,
teaches me to touch the love being of God herself.

Woman God of Truth,
lead me into the newness of unfaith.
Breathe with me through this lightsome darkness.
Lead me through the nameless nights.
Open my spirit to
new love
new clarity
new fidelity
new truth,
and again,
new darkness.

What joy to be human
and know ever and ever again
the nameless God,
she of the nameless nights.

(Hadewijch of Brabant)

Seven Ways of Loving

Love is love is love.
A rose is a rose is a rose.
This was my pedestrian musing,
as I trod the ways of life
with leaden feet and weighted spirit.
In my cynical been-there, done-that attitude,
all the mystical talk of love seemed trite,
beyond reason, ephemeral,
too holy for twenty-first century mortals.

And then I met Beatrice.
'There are seven ways of loving', she said,
'and here they are.'
And here is the hook:
these are not for the holy
but for every thing, every one, every person,
    every animal, bird and tree.
We are living in love,
so let us enjoy it.

Her one problem:
How can the finite love the infinite?
But she answers her own question, as mystics tend to do,
how can the finite not love the infinite?
Every love says this:
I want the proximity of the infinite.
Every love is a love of the infinite.
Every love dreams of an infinity of love:
this is the nature of loving.

And so she goes through her seven ways:
through longing, acting, trusting,
through bribery, begging, and aching,
when love weakens;

and then peace and serenity,
and freedom of conscience arrive.
when all things infinite and finite meet.

God the infinite, infinite Mother, infinite Father,
meets the infinity of the depths of humanity
and all is one.
She is in her element
like the stereotypical birds of the air
and the stereotypical fishes in the sea.
and, knowing this, they tell me,
Beatrice often burst out laughing
right in the middle of prayers.

And then the really miraculous happens:
she discovers her element not in the holy stereotypical places,
but with the real birds,
with the real fish,
with the real people,
with all those aching for love.

She enters her real element:
the daily intimacies of loving
each one, every one,
seven times and seven times and seven times,
and seven times a day,
she is embraced by Love.

(Beatrice of Nazareth)

Lover Woman God

Have you heard the singing,
the song of God
serenading the universe?

On this breaking spring day,
the God-song hums,
the air is alive.
The garden shimmers in song,
As a symphony composed
just for me.

O lovely rose on the thorn
O lovely bee in the honey
O pure dove in your being
O glorious sun in your setting
O full moon in your course
From you,
I your God,
will never turn away.

From break of day
To fall of night
This God-song
Sings in my heart.

(Mechtilde of Magdeburg)

Gifts of Friendship

*Farewell**

And when Hiltigarde,
the queen wife of Charlemagne
importuned her to stay a few days longer
Leoba refused but,
embracing her friend rather more affectionately than usual,
she kissed her on the mouth,
the forehead and the eyes
and took leave of her with these words:
'Farewell for evermore,
my dearly beloved lady and sister;
farewell most precious half of my soul.
May Christ, our Creator and Redeemer
grant that we shall meet again without shame
on the day of judgement.
Nevermore on this earth shall we enter each other's presence.'

(Life of Leoba)

*Our Special Friends**

We love everyone with a general love,
but God sometimes gives us also a special love
to love more intimately one person,
who then becomes a close particular friend.
This is so that we can support each other more faithfully.
For the love with which I love myself,
that is the love with which I love my friend.

This is how it is with very dear friends:
their loving affection makes them two bodies with one soul,
because love transforms us into what we love.
And if these souls are made one
nothing can be hidden from them.
Don't let cowardice keep you from loving.

But even more,
God has so identified himself with us
that our love for one another truly binds us to God as well.
Jesus told me:
'I have put you among others
so that you can do for them
what you cannot do for me ...
Love them without any concern for thanks,
and without looking for any profit for yourself,
and whatever you do for them,
I will consider done for me.'

(Catherine of Siena)

God and My Friends

My soul is sick again,
and again I know why:
I have been putting my friends to the test.

Why, O God of friendship, is love so tough?
Why do we dance through this ballet of seeking and rejecting?
Why such faith hardness
and heart stubbornness?
Why such soul sluggish?

Once a gardener said to me:
'The plants want to grow,
Leave them be.'
I have learned this about my friends:
love wants to grow,
wants to blossom, wants to flourish.

Yes there is pruning
and mulching
and feeding and enriching.
But we must trust the soil
the deep tangle of distrust and guilt
only weakens the roots.
So know this:
Love is mysterious presence
Love is the face of God
Love is the key to the abyss
Love is the prober of depths
Love is the face of your friend
Love is where God is.

(Hadewijch of Brabant)

Beyond Silence

Ego Clamor Validus

Why, why, why, O God,
    does the voice of a woman so distress them?
My voice is the one you have given me:
Even my name says it, Hrotsvith, *clamor validus*,
I am the strong voice of Gandersheim.

The men know and own their voice:
And I?
I sought the monastic safety of Gandersheim
and here, Oh joy, my abbess, Gerberga,
urges me to speak:
'So much needs to be said about women', she said.

She told me to read all that had been written about women,
the lies, deceptions, distortions,
all their lives turned to ridicule for men's pleasure,
and through men's fear.
'Change all that,' she said to me, 'tell the story of women.'

And so, my God, I use my voice, the *clamor validus*,
which is your gift to me to tell the story of women.
I will write, O God, of women's true selves,
of women as you see them,
as you created them,
as you speak to them,

The men say to me:
'Excuse your sex. Women do not speak like this,
a woman's knowledge is inferior.'
But I am the strong voice of Gandersheim,
and I do not need to excuse what God has given
and Gerberga has commanded.

So, O God, sprinkle my mind with dew,
and moisten gently with your love the dark recesses of my mind.
Do not let the voice you gave me
grow rusty from neglect.

You direct me to Terence, poet of the Romans,
pagan indeed, but it is he who said:
Nihil humanum alienum mihi.
Nothing that is human is alien to me:
This, O God, is the path I will follow.

He wrote of womanly wiles:
I will change that and write of the women I know,
their strength, holiness, goodness, courage, hospitality,
and above all, their ability to face themselves,
to remake their lives,
to know the truth of themselves
created and ever-loved by you.

I want my pen to praise your greatness
in the greatness of women.
I want to urge women to move beyond despair,
that sin which is the bane of womankind.
We have been told so often that we are nothing,
that despair seems the easy road.
I want women to know it is not so.
We are made for great things.

I want women to cease the pretence of being voiceless
and to raise their voice in womanly words of praise and hope.

I want, O God, to be the one,
who with flinty spark can set the whole sea alight.
I want all women to say without excuse:
Ego clamor validus.

(Hrotswith of Gandersheim)

When I Was Five

Now I begin to know why I have been struggling.
Now it is coming clear to me why I have always been a little ill,
never my true, lively, energetic self,
always battling uphill, gasping for breath,
throat constricted and lungs flailing.

I am beginning to remember when I was five.

Then it was that I was first conscious of a power of holy insight
running through my being.
At five, I was clear-eyed, open-eared, full-voiced.
When I was five, they thought it was a childish game.

Now I know that it was you, O God, nourishing my child's spirit.
Ever since childhood,
in the marrow of my bones and the veins of my flesh,
I feel withered.
I am aching to speak,
but a woman's voice is, they say, the voice of demons.
What do we need to hear from a woman, but evil?

And then, finally, my friends wearied of my excuses.
Volmar and Richardis said enough:
Speak!

I have found a way of speaking,
not in trance, not in heavenly vision, not in mysterious sounds;
I speak through the power of story.
I write pictures, I make visible in paint
that which I see in my prayer.

Now they call me mystic, visionary, holy Abbess;
but it is I, the same Hildegarde.
Nothing in me has changed
except that I have found my voice.

All I ever wanted was to speak God:
They speak of a single Trinity:
I see Trinities everywhere.
They speak of a changeless God:
I see God in light and discord.
They speak of a distant God,
far removed from the world of Bingen:
I see God here in my garden,
outside my window, rising in the juicy sap of the spring plants.

They speak of a God who thunders:
but I have met a God
who soars and floats and ripples in the moist air.
And again I know:
I am a feather on the breath of God.

(Hildegarde of Bingen)

Rivers of Fire

Again I am in turmoil.
Should I speak or must I be silent?
I feel like a gnarled old tree, withered and crooked and flaky.
All the stories of the years are written on my branches.
The sap is gone, the voice is dead.

But I long to make again a sacred sound.
I want to sound out God
I want to be a young juicy, sap-running tree
So that I can sing God as God knows how.

O God, you gentle viridity
O Mary, honeycomb of life
O Jesus, hidden in sweetness as flowing honey,
Release my voice again.

I have sweetness to share.
I have stories to tell.
I have God to announce.
I have green life to celebrate.
I have rivers of fire to ignite.

(Hildegarde of Bingen).

Seeking the Ways of God

God, I go east:
You call me to begin in light
my journey toward you.
Let this light be in my life
the brilliant sun of justice.

God I go north:
You turn my face inward
to mark the darkness and coldness of my own heart.
Melt the ice that can encase my mind.
Unseal the frostiness of my struggling heart.

God I go south:
You open to me the lightsome paths of wisdom.
Teach me to choose well
to befriend the spirit of choice.

God I go west:
You point me again to the Scriptures
where I can meet your Word
on the highways and byways of Life.
Open my eyes to the flashing forth
of these brilliant rays of light.
Go with me:
I go with you.

(Hildegarde of Bingen)

For Mary

One Woman's Life

All the blessings of God are seen in one woman's life.
All the blessings in this woman's life
    are seen in every woman's life.
She is Mary, Woman of Nazareth, mother of Jesus.

The first red of daylight reveals her
and draws me to the depths of dawn.
The budded green branch shouts aloud her name
and promises me a time of hope and power.

The lucid stream, flowing and concealing nothing,
but adding beauty to stones in the rippling light,
calls to me to look through the ripples of life
to the clear lucidity of God's inner being.
And in that light I see Mary:
One woman
Every woman.

(Hildegard of Bingen)

I Want Radiance

What Mary says to me is clarity:
I am muddled, confused, mumbling.
Mary, free me from my destructive ways,
I want your radiance.

What Mary says to me is 'Be radical':
Root yourself in the rich soil of humanity,
Your body, like that of a lily, is the container of joy.
Be deeply green and dazzlingly white.
Be radiant.

What Mary says to me is flight
the soaring flight of birds in song.
Look up, listen, drink it in.
God is overflying the world
from beyond the furthest stars.
In Mary's arms God comes
greeting us eternally
with a kiss of heavenly peace.
Be flight.

(Hildegarde of Bingen)

Magnificat

strong woman
woman on the edge
woman of the open spaces
dwelling in the empty places
woman on the edge

she is listening for a distant song
even a single word
she is hoping to hear the very voice
of God

she is digging in her garden
she is looking for roots
her fingers probe the damp cool earth
the place where life begins
she still believes in beauty
and miracles and promises
she has faith in seeds

her heart is open
she longs to sing a song of victory
to dance with light feet
among the flowers crushed and trampled
to heal

she is longing to feel her feet on the ground
her roots sinking deeply
into the dark soft earth she is looking for a revolution
she is aching for grace
she is seeking the very face
of God

and grace pays an unexpected visit
in woman-form, a wise woman
with laughter-lines carved round her eyes

and holes in her boots
a touch of silver in her hair
wise woman listens and knows and sees

then she hears once more the old song
familiar chords
which strike deep and true
and echo throughout her body
her heart her womb
the place where life begins
she hears once more the old song
out of the silence
the emptiness

she didn't know today was the day
to rewrite her story
she is weaving colours and images and memories
into a whole
she too is source, and giver of life
capax dei
she is poet and dancer and prophet and mother
embracing joy
dreaming and birthing and sinking into the warm soil

she is rediscovering the colour blue
blue, born of fire
born in the first waters
welling up from the heart of the earth
she is rediscovering blue
in the first morning glory on the vine

she is learning to sing a triumphal song
to dance through the garden with feather-light feet
learning to heal
she is not afraid to become
she is a strong woman
a woman on the edge
singing in the open spaces
dancing in the empty places
strong woman
woman on the edge

(Elsie Gerber)

Shimmering

Hail, O shimmering girl,
Essence of lily.

Hail, O raiment of Christ
Brilliance of blossom.

Hail, O chord of joy
Heart of all harmony.

Hail, O grassland of delight
Moistness of green.

Hail, O glimmer of dawn
Blush of the approaching day.

Hail, O Mary
Highly-chosen,
Everywoman,
Heart of humanity.

(Hildegarde of Bingen)

Creation

Love the Land

You, O endlessly creating and creative God,
have given the lovely green land into our keeping,
but you never gave us power over it.
'Don't think,' you said, 'that you can do with it what you wish.'
We sow the seed, but without your grace,
that living mysterious sap of life,
the seed will not bear fruit.

For it is you who sprinkle the dew,
You who pour down the rain,
You who moisten the earth,
now with tears of joy, now with gladness, now with sorrow.
You produce the warmth of the sun.
You are the light which acts like a magnet,
to draw all living things towards you.

God of wisdom, you have given me the power
to pour words into a person's ear;
but it is you, not I, that changes a person's heart.
So it is with the land.
God of the Land and the People,
send down on us
the dew of grace and fruitfulness,
the rain of tears and longing and reaching upwards,
the moisture of softening and cajoling,
the richness of maturing and persevering,
the warmth of the spirit of energy and love.

Be the running sap of our lives.
Clothe us in viridity, in greenness.
Tend the budding branches,
garland us with the blossoms of beauty.
Bind us together with the vines of compassion.
Make us into waving fronds
so that we may dance before you in joy.

With you among us, we are holy people.
Within your embrace, the land is holy.
Afloat in your love,
all created things live your praise.
We hear, we see, we are in awe
And we give thanks.

(Hildegarde of Bingen)

Body-Talk: A Litany

Body who are you?

I am your friend and closest partner,
I am mother and father and often child.
Always I am you lover and spouse.
I found God in myself and I loved her, I loved her fiercely.

Body who are you?

I am the truth-teller:
I witness to your unknown and often unloved self.
I am the faithful messenger and recorder of your memories,
    your power.
I remember, I etch into skin and bone your hurts,
    your needs, your limits.
I found God in myself and I loved her, I loved her fiercely.

Body who are you?

I am the story of your life.
I am the text where all can read this story.
I am the stored wisdom of the joy and hurts
of all the generations before you.
I found God in myself and I loved her, I loved her fiercely.

Body who are you?

I am the gift-giver.
Through me you live and move in God's creation.
Through me you have your vital link
with the rejoicing, groaning, travailing, beautiful universe.
I found God in myself and I loved her, I loved her fiercely.

Body who are you?

I am your partner in stress and pain;
I carry your suffering.
I partner your spirit in bearing the barbs of hurt.
I found God in myself and I loved her, I loved her fiercely.

Body who are you?

I am your partner in joy and delight.
Through me you express the laughter and love
that link you to your deepest self and your deepest love.
I found God in myself and I loved her, I loved her fiercely.

Body who are you?

I am the frontier you have barely explored.
I am always in touch with messages of invitation:
Come explore this new land.
I am the manifestation of the miracle that is you.
I am the microcosm of the universe in which you live.
I found God in myself and I loved her, I loved her fiercely.

Body who are you?

I am the visible means through which you communicate,
with eyes that see and weep and shine,
with ears that heed and ignore and learn,
with hands that reach and heal and hurt and caress,
with nose that drinks in the fragrance of hope
    and the acidity of despair,
with feet that run and tumble and falter and race.
I am who you are.
I am how you live.
I am always with you.
I found God in myself and I loved her, I loved her fiercely.

Body who are you?

I am the ground of your being.
In me all is made one.
I found God in myself and I loved her, I loved her fiercely.

(After Ntozake Shange)[2]

---

2. The refrain, 'I found God in myself ...' is from a play by Ntozake
Shange. Other phrases in this poem have lingered in my mind for
years, but I have forgotten their origin.

The Voice of Earth Speaking God's Presence

Earth teach me stillness
as the grasses are stilled with light.

Earth teach me honest suffering
as old stones suffer with memory.

Earth teach me humility
as blossoms are humble with beginning.

Earth teach me caring
as the mother bird nestles her young.

Earth teach me gentleness
as the deer walks softly through the forest.

Earth teach me courage
as the tree which stands straight alone.

Earth teach me limitation
as the ant who crawls along the ground.

Earth teach me freedom
as the lark who sings and soars.

Earth teach me joy
as the bee delighting in the nectar of life.

Earth teach me resignation
as the cycle of life turns and turns.

Earth teach me about the regeneration of life
as the seed rises after being scattered and buried.

Earth teach me playfulness
as the otter rolling with the river currents.

Earth teach me to be generous
as the rains and snow water the soil.

Earth teach me to remember kindness
as the blossoms turn rejoicing towards the sun.

Earth teach me good suffering
as the land struggles with ingenuity to survive our greed.

Earth teach me gratitude
as the soil begins a new journey toward the autumnal harvest.

Earth teach me to know the Author of Life
as I daily gaze in wonder
    at the marvellous mysterious sustenance of all creation.

(Anonymous)[3]

---

3. I have been unable to trace the origin of this poem which I seem to
have always known. I have re-written several of the phrases.

Autumn

It is late Autumn and
I take my camera to the garden.
The reel is almost full;
I use it up
taking the picture of a
small insignificant shrub.

What a surprise when
it turns out to be
the best of the lot:

The leaves are pale,
yellow-green
with decaying stains;
but brilliant black berries
eyes from the dying sun
take over.
The Crone decays
but leaves new life
in her trail.

(Brid Murphy)

Song of the Universe

What song is this
    echoing through the ages
    etching creative paths
    from celestial stars to conscious minds?

Who is this virtuous maestro
    gifting all life forms
    with innate spiritual song
        seeking relationships and harmony?

What love is this
    exhibiting delightful and infinite scores
    satiating senses with the song of the universe
        – beauty, harmony, transparency?

Who is this perfect rendition
    whose life, death and resurrection
    reconciles discord and crooked paths
        restoring rhythms for life?

Who am I? but one aria
    captivated by this heavenly ensemble
    begging
        the grace to forever sing in harmony my song
        that I may forever celebrate and dance
    the Song of the Universe.

(Shirley Anne Majeau FCJ)

Sweet-Smelling God

I am the secret Fire in everything,
And everything smells like
Me.
The living breathe in my sweet perfume
and they breathe out praise of me.
They never die
because I am their Life.

I flame out
intense Godly life
over the shining fields of corn.
I glow in the shimmer of the fire's embers.
I burn in the sun and the moon and the stars.
My secret life breathes in the wind
and holds all things together soulfully.
This is God's voice.

(Hildegarde of Bingen).

The Youth of Age

Praying at Seventy

All my life, it now seems to me,
I have had clear sight of God.
Like currents of air, spirits gliding upward,
I have been in flight.

The clouds form and reform,
they race across the sky and swell in stillness, all aglowing,
and they say: Remember God!

As my physical eyes fail,
my inner eyes open to wonder.
As my bodily ears strain,
my God-antennae are instantly alert
and announce: She, your God, is here.

As my brain is sometimes befuddled,
my heart leaps in elation at the robin's antics.
As my feet stumble, my spirit races ahead:
Come on, Come on, there is so much more.

As my hands grow numb, and sometimes sore,
my touch grows softer, sensitive, more grace-filled.
My senses may dim,
but my whole being seems alive
and shouts: 'Live it up.'

I seem now to be bathed in light.
I say to myself:
'Now I am living in the shadow of the Living Light'

I used to worry about sin;
now I have no time for this.
When I pick up the Scriptures,
the light streams out at me
The words tremble with life,
and shout: 'Abundant Life.'

My memory is memorising:
all the strands are being drawn together.
I can now say:
'I see, I hear, I know, I smile, I love.'

I see new words, hear new music, know in deeper tones,
I smile at my dreams, I love with the trees.

I see bright flames coming from human lips.
I see rippling water flowing in endless light.
No container on earth can keep this flowing.

All my life is now here in the palm of my hand:
I am child, maid, woman, crone.
I live it all, now more fully.

How can I now describe my lightsome life?
I see
I yearn yet.

(Hildegarde of Bingen)

Crone Times

Eighty is not as old as it used to be;
the crone is coming into her own again.

***From wise woman
Ban-Dia
Whose word brought life,
New Birth-

To decline
when the male god took over

And the culling of women began
in centuries of burning,
when witches became evil,

Which in time
Gave rise to Oxford
Calling her 'an ugly old hag'

To the growing certainty
that God / dess is
alive and well
and we crones
called to be the
fulfilment of the certainty
that 'I came that you may
have Life and have it more abundantly.'

Now the sky is the limit
and the magnificent horizons of the sea
call us to enter into the fullness
of the Ocean.

(Brid Murphy)

The Flame of Anger

Letter to the Bishop

You ask why I disobey you, my bishop;
I answer in a spirit of prayer,
as I hope you did too in addressing me.
I, the Abbess, disobey, and all my sisters choose to disobey,
because in such obedience is only darkness.
In our disobedience is light for our spirits,
so has God shown us.

I am not just disobedient,
I am outraged.
A thunderstorm of outrage shakes my soul.
In God's truth I say to you:
'You are wrong and we are right.'

We are obeying Christ,
We are following Christ,
We choose not to insult Christ,
As obeying you would force us to do.

Because of what you call our disobedience,
you have forbidden us to sing our psalms.
You have deprived us of the Food of Life.
You have cut off the streams of life, the sacramental graces.

The convent now is silent.
Our songs have ceased, as you asked.
We faint from lack of sustenance, as you command,
(We are not, after all, unreasonable);
but I can still speak to you for my sisters.
and this is what I have to report:

As we at first succumbed to sadness,
God spoke to us and said:
'This is not good.'
How can you be forbidden to come to me – even by bishops?
God, your Excellency, has told me to tell you this.

God said, Listen to the psalms saying:
'Let everything that has breath praise God'
And you command us to be silent.

God said: 'Tell the Bishop he is living by outward reality
I want you to turn to inner reality.'

So, for our part,
though still silent,
we have turned all our energies inward.
We have directed our inner selves toward God;
we sing in our hearts.
Our eyes greet one another and smile in song.
Our lips beam with God's silent praises, louder than any hymn.
There is not one outward sound,
but the house rings with the energy of our praise.

The angels seem to have come among us,
their sweet souvenirs of heaven can be heard in the halls.
The holy prophets of God walk the orchard paths with us,
the heavenly harpists have come to dwell in Bingen.

We do not touch the musical instruments with our hands,
but we breathe on them as we pass,
and what heavenly music we hear in our hearts.
We obey you where you are in outward reality
but in our hearts, we walk with God, and God with us.

God told me to tell you this also:
Beware of closing the mouths of those who sing God's praises.
'Who dares to destring the harp of heaven?' God asked me.
'Only the devil,' I whispered.

Ask yourself, O bishop, whose side are you on?

As for us, we sing in silence,
and we have discovered that
our soul is symphonic.

And I heard a voice saying:
'Who created heaven?' God
'Who opens heaven to the faithful ones?' God
'Who is like God?' Nobody.
So, O bishop, do not resist God,
lest you really discover the power of God.
With respect I write and in God's name.
Abbess Hildegarde.

(Hildegarde of Bingen, aged 80)

Hell? No

'Go to hell,' she shouted,
her ninety-year-old voice
hoarse with anger.
I winced as the phone crashed in my ear.

And then I smiled at the wasted execration,
since, having read Julian,
I no longer believe in hell.
And all will be well
And all will be well
And all manner of thing will be well.
Even angry aunts.

(Julian of Norwich)

Staying the Course

God With God
I want to grow up to be God with God. (Hadewijch of Brabant)

It was Pentecost,
I had a vision at dawn and
I though I was going mad.
All winter I had felt as if I were in exile;
I wanted God, whole and entire.

'You have to grow up,' God told me,
'Grow up to be God with God.
To let everything come and go without grief;
if you want God, get ready for this.

Then your humanity will image God,
as Jesus did.
Then God will look at you
and see God
Then Eucharist will be your home.
You will not know where you end and God begins,
and where God ends and you begin.
you will be God with God.'

So whether it is wintry exile,
or Pentecost abundance,
then I will always know
God is closer to me
than I am to myself.

(Hadewijch of Brabant)

Living in Infinity

Spirit of the deeps,
You call out to me to test your infinity.
Mark your steps, you say
Start out slowly,
because once started, there is no end
but joy.
It is like a woman in labour:
once the first step is taken,
there is no stopping it,
a long slow drawing out
of the deep mysteries of life.

This is God's pedagogy of time:
Time moving relentlessly,
Time standing still in the midst of movement,
Time vanishing as mystery takes hold,
Time emptied even of longing.

Live in this infinity of time.
Let mystery meet mystery,
something deep within will respond.
And then,
where else can I feel at home?
Spirit of the deeps,
reach, touch, draw, hold.

(Hadewijch of Brabant)

Lie Down in the Fire

What, you ask, does it mean
to live a Godly life?
It means this one thing:
lie down in the fire.
Only there, at the fiery heart,
will you find her.
Only there will you see and taste and know
the flowing being of God,
She in you and you in her.
Lie down in the fire
Make it your home
Flow with its flowing
Burn in its burning.
Then, moulded together
fire in fire
love in love
you will be
God with God.

(Mechtilde of Magdeburg)

Help, O God

Be my honour, God,
my joy
my beauty
my consolation in sorrow
my counsel in uncertainty
my defence in everything unfair
my patience in problems
my abundance in poverty
my food in fasting
my sleep in vigilance
and my therapy in weakness.

(Gertrude the Great, *Incandescence*, p 20)

Sound Advice

Here's some advice for everyday life:
When you pray, be humble.
When you confess, be honest.
When you do penance, do it indefatigably.
When you eat, be sensible.
When you sleep, be disciplined.
When you're alone, be faithful.
When you're with others, be discreet.
When someone teaches you good manners, be receptive.
When someone reprimands you for your mistakes, be patient.
When you do something bad, ask forgiveness immediately.
When you're full of self-absorbed pride,
    fear for the health of your soul.
When you're sad, trust in God completely.
When you're doing manual work, work hard,
Because hard work drives off every evil thought.

(Mechtilde of Magdeburg)

Going Home

The Race Is On

What a life she had lived, our Macrina,
owner of thousands of acres and hundreds of slaves.
And then she heard your voice floating in from the desert.
All was changed in an instant.

We always knew that our mother
    was given her secret name before birth.
We think it was Thecla,
    the virgin companion of the apostle Paul.
But our mother said it was her life that mattered, not her name,
and so we, her brother Basil and I, knew her as Macrina,
    our dear Macrina.

And now, in her final act of love,
she is racing toward you, O God,
and as in life, so in death,
Macrina is clear about how her final moments will be lived.

As I sit here beside her, I remember her life:
How she freed all her slaves,
Sold the land to feed the poor,
Founded convents,
Devoured the gospels,
Always worked with her hands.
I remember those hands, never at rest,
Calming, healing, teaching, baking, planting, building, writing
And even now they are moving.
Now that her voice is stilled,
it is with her hands that she prays:
clutching, waving, caressing my hand,
stroking her lips, reaching toward her sisters.

I remember her strong and vibrant faith.
For a while, Basil and Peter and I, her brothers,
and even her mother feared her.
She cajoled, persuaded, reasoned, even bullied,
until we too heard your desert voice, O God.

I know now, O God, that the dreams
    that have been troubling my soul
were dreams of Macrina,
drawing me towards her
for this final farewell.

As that moment draws near,
I can hear the choir singing the evening prayer.
She looked her last goodbye to me.
Her final moments were for you alone,
the companion God of her life.
Her words came softly:
'Open for me, O God, the path of resurrection.
Reshape my being with your grace
so that your hand of love may encircle my life.
Lead me, O God, along the shining path
to the place of my refreshment.
Bathe me in the waters of relaxation,
for I have feared you, but now fear no more.
Forgive my sins.
Show me your face.'
And she was gone.

(Gregory of Nyssa, describing his sister's last hours)

The Magnet

God, I still have a great fear
as to the way my soul
will pass from my body.
Then the Lord said to me:
'It shall be thus:
I will draw my breath
and your soul shall come to me
as a needle to a magnet.'

(Mechtilde of Magdeburg)

Divining Death
(For Connor)

Our first visit home
after the amputations,
he wheel-chair bound
learning to live a short-circuited life.
Family and friends gathered in my mother's house,
as we chattered of ordinary things and ordinary events.

One friend had brought her child,
her blond, sun-freckled son of three years.
In a sudden conversation lull
the small clear voice asked,
'Where are his legs?
Why is he kneeling in the chair?'

A rush of adult explanation followed
about pain and doctors and hospitals and all better now.
The child seemed content;
the conversation continued,
more intent now on not noticing.

Then movement:
the small blond child, like a ray of sun after storm
solemnly crossed the room
and planted a kiss on each ravaged limb,
a sudden impulse of pure grace
helping him deal with the mystery of pain;
an anointing, an unction,
bridging the gap between shattered limbs and emptiness.

Some time later, too short a time,
we lay together again
thinking together out loud
divining death, our featureless future.

We had wondered, Aquinas-like,
    about the great emptiness ahead,
the whereness and whyness and whatness of simply not being,
and were not much comforted.

We had remembered Mechtilde
and her magnetic image of life attracting life
in effortless wonder,
and were drawn somewhat further into mystery.

'Perhaps,' he said, smiles lightening his voice,
'it will be like Connor's kiss.'
One sudden impulse of sheer grace,
bridging the gap between
presence and absence,
between life and after-life.
A last anointing,
An extreme unction

That summer child's kiss
brought joy and laughing memory,
where the great Aquinas
and the mystical Mechtilde
had left the gap yawning still.

'Amen,' we said,
'let it only be so.'

Jubilus

My husband lay dying on the bed
and I, fingers entwined in his,
lay stretched out beside him.
It was the deep, silent hour,
no noises intruded except
the accustomed ticking of household gadgets.

We had talked on and off all evening,
knowing that it was no longer
months and weeks,
but days and even hours.
Our time together was slipping away.

And then,
'Let's sing,' he said
And, as one,
We broke into the old favourite:
'For you are beautiful,
And I have loved you dearly,
more dearly than the spoken word can tell.'

We sang at full strength,
as if entering into some great anthem,
voices full of laughter and joy,
spirits rising to the truth of love,
giving way gladly to the mysteries of life and loss.

And for that brief moment,
we knew Jubilus.

(Jubilus: the effortless, often hours-long singing experienced by
some mystics, especially when close to death)